P9-CEB-619

EXECUTION OF LOUNT AND MATTHEWS [date and artist unknown].
Public Archives of Canada, C–1242.

THE REBELLION
IN UPPER CA